# My First Chess Book

Katie Daynes

Chess consultant: Sarah Hegarty

Illustrated by The Boy Fitz Hammond
Designed by Michael Hill

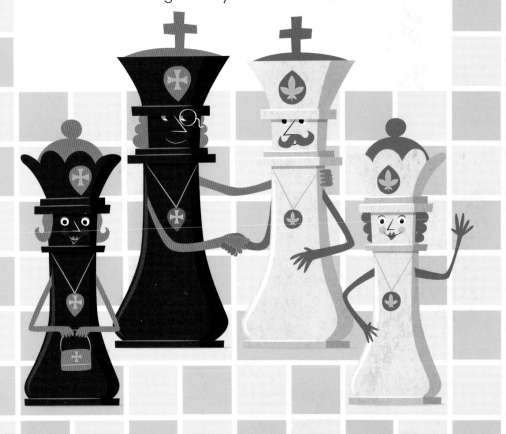

# Contents

# Playing chess

Chess has been enjoyed for hundreds of years by people of all ages. All you need to play a game is a chess set and a basic grasp of the rules.

This book will teach you all you need to start playing.

## Who can I play?

• Challenge a friend or family member to a game of chess.

• You could join a chess club in your school or in your local area and play people there.

• You can also play against a computer or online.

• After you've had some practice, you could try entering a competition.

Chess is a game where children really can beat grown-ups!

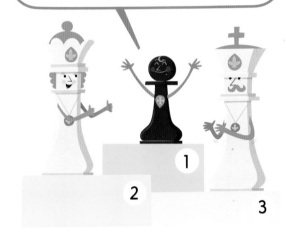

1

2

3

## Chess online

For online games, puzzles and tips, go to the Usborne Quicklinks website at www.usborne.com/quicklinks and type in the title of this book.

We recommend children are supervised on the internet.

# Chess armies

Chess is a game for two players. One player controls an army of white pieces and the other controls an army of black pieces. The pieces have different names and different ways of moving.

Meet the army

We're the PAWNS.

There are eight of us.

We're the ROOKS.
There are two of us.

Neigh! We're the two KNIGHTS.

We're the two BISHOPS.

I'm the QUEEN.

And I'm the KING.

# The battlefield

The battlefield is a board made up of 64 squares. Half the squares are light and half of them are darker. Here you can see which squares the pieces go on at the start of every game.

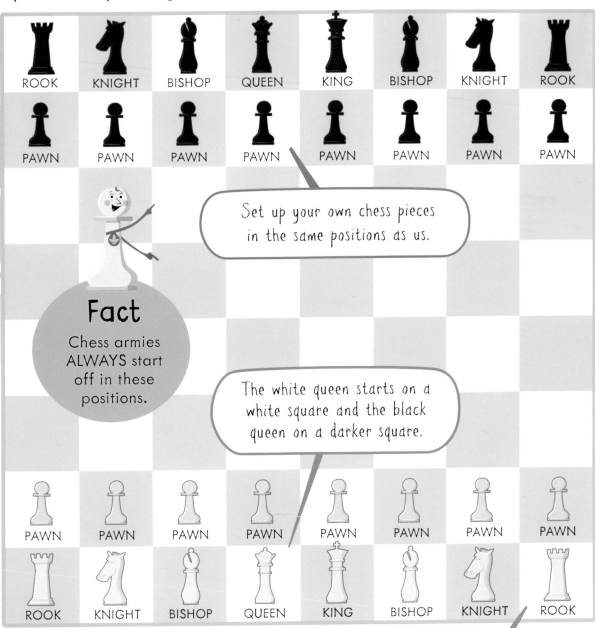

ROOK  KNIGHT  BISHOP  QUEEN  KING  BISHOP  KNIGHT  ROOK

PAWN  PAWN  PAWN  PAWN  PAWN  PAWN  PAWN  PAWN

Set up your own chess pieces in the same positions as us.

## Fact

Chess armies ALWAYS start off in these positions.

The white queen starts on a white square and the black queen on a darker square.

PAWN  PAWN  PAWN  PAWN  PAWN  PAWN  PAWN  PAWN

ROOK  KNIGHT  BISHOP  QUEEN  KING  BISHOP  KNIGHT  ROOK

## The aim

To win the game you must use your army to trap the enemy king.

The corner square on your right should always be white.

5

# The rules

Here are the basic rules you must follow in a game of chess.

## Taking turns

• The player with the white army always starts.

• Then it's the player with the black army's turn.

• Keep taking turns.

• Each turn is called a move. You only move one piece each turn, onto a new square.

After you.

Thank you.

I can't move yet.

I can.

## The moves

The pieces have their own special ways of moving.

There are different patterns for different pieces. This book will explain them to you.

Making the right moves

## Top tip

Take one piece at a time and learn how it moves, before you play a full game.

# Capturing

You can capture an enemy piece by POUNCING on it.

Put your piece on the enemy's square, and take the enemy piece off the board.

Got you! That's my square now.

I've already been captured.

Grrr. I'll get you next time!

# Winning

You win the game by trapping the enemy king.

If there's no way for him to escape, then you say 'Checkmate'.

Well done – you've won.

## Fact

There are more possible moves in a chess game than there are grains of sand on all the beaches in the world.

Checkmate!

I can't escape. You win.

That means there are BILLIONS of moves you can make!

# Pawn soldiers

Just don't call them prawns...

We're the front line of your army.

We're ready to fight the enemy.

## Marching forward

Pawns can only move forwards – one or two squares on their first move, then one square at a time after that.

My army starts at the top and moves down.

## Fact

In pictures of chess games, the black army is normally shown at the top and the white army at the bottom.

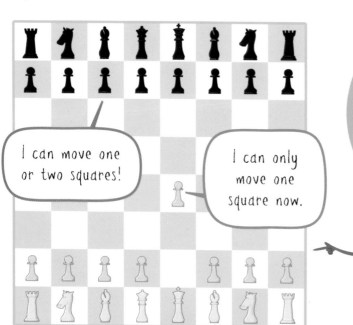

I can move one or two squares!

I can only move one square now.

My army starts here and moves up.

# Capturing diagonally

Pawns are the only chess pieces that move differently to capture a piece.

When a piece gets in front of a pawn, its way is blocked.

To capture a piece, a pawn must move one *diagonal* step forward.

We're both stuck!

Got you!

# Reaching the other side

If a pawn reaches the far side of the board, it can turn into any other piece (except for a king or another pawn).

This is called pawn **promotion**. You take the pawn off the board and put the other piece in its place.

Pick me! I'm the most powerful...

Ooo, who shall I be?

## Top tip

If you haven't got a spare piece, use something else. An upside-down rook can be a queen.

# A pawn game

Before learning about the other chess pieces, try out
your pawn moves in a pawn game for two players.

## How to play

• Line up the pawns in their starting positions.

• Take turns to move your pawns. (White moves first.)

• The first player to reach the other side of the board wins.

Remember, we move one
or two spaces forward
on our first move...

...and only one
space forward
after that.

A pawn straight in front
will block our way.

To capture another pawn,
we move diagonally.

# Strengths

Pawns work well together, attacking and defending. They become more valuable as they near the other side of the board.

Nearly there...

I'm going to be a queen!

Great teamwork, pawns.

# Weaknesses

Pawns can't move backwards and they're not very strong on their own, so think before you push one forwards.

## Fact

'Pawn' comes from an old word for 'foot soldier' (a soldier without a horse to ride on).

I guess I'll have to walk.

Hey, you're in my way.

Help, I'm all alone.

# Jumping knights

## Up and over

Knights are the only chess pieces that can jump over other pieces.
See how the black knight moves out of trouble in the pictures below.

# L shapes

Knights always move in L shapes, in any direction – two squares forward and one to the side.

There are eight squares this black knight can move to...

## Fact

Knights are the only pieces that don't move in a single straight line.

We don't capture the pieces we jump over – only the pieces we land on.

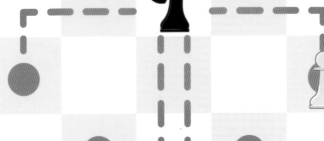

Please don't capture me!

## Top tip

Pretend you're a knight next time you're on a checked floor and try out your moves!

# A knight game

Try this knight game for one or two players.

• Place a knight on its starting square.

• Choose a square in the middle of the board.

• Try to reach that square in as few moves as possible (only using the knight's L-shaped moves).

• If you're playing with two players, take turns to move. The first one there is the winner.

Let's aim for this square.

OK. You chose the square so I'll go first.

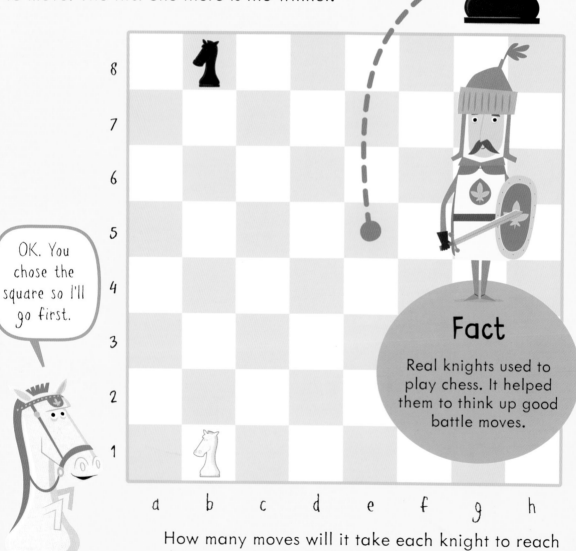

## Fact

Real knights used to play chess. It helped them to think up good battle moves.

How many moves will it take each knight to reach the square marked above? Who will get there first?

# Strengths

Knights move well in a crowd because they can jump over other pieces.
They're really good at surprise attacks.
A knight can threaten two enemy pieces at the same time.

# Weaknesses

Knights sometimes get stuck at the edge of the board and they can't capture pieces that are right next to them.

## Top tip

Remember this saying: knights on the rim are dim.

# Pointy bishops

We're the ones with the pointy heads.

One bishop only moves on the darker squares...

...and the other only moves on white squares.

## Zigzagging

Bishops move forwards or backwards in diagonal lines across empty spaces.

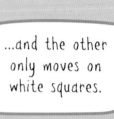

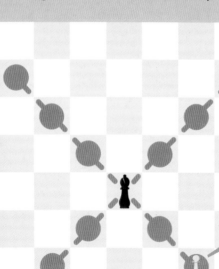

This bishop can stop on any square along these lines.

He can capture me and stop on this square, but he can't go past me.

## Fact

Elephants from the Indian army were used instead of bishops in old versions of chess.

# Strengths

Bishops are great at covering both sides of the board and at moving long distances.

Uh oh. That bishop's on the attack. Which piece will he go for?

Aghh, he's taken our rook.

Whew. That was a close escape.

# Weaknesses

Bishops can get trapped behind pawns – and they can't switch from white squares to dark squares (or dark to white).

I'm stuck. The dark squares are blocked.

## Top tip

Move your pawns first, then your knights and bishops.

# Towering rooks

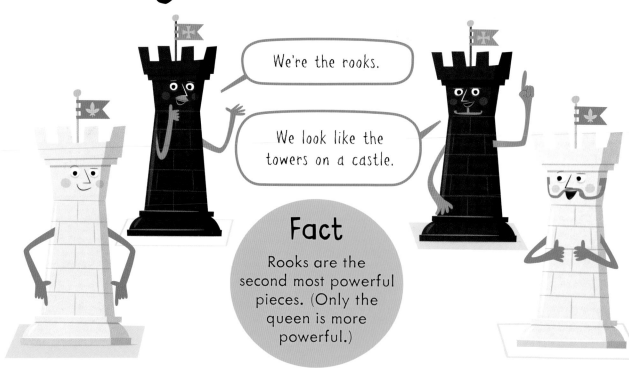

We're the rooks.

We look like the towers on a castle.

## Fact

Rooks are the second most powerful pieces. (Only the queen is more powerful.)

## Straight moves

Rooks move in straight lines along empty squares – forwards, backwards or side to side, but NOT diagonally.

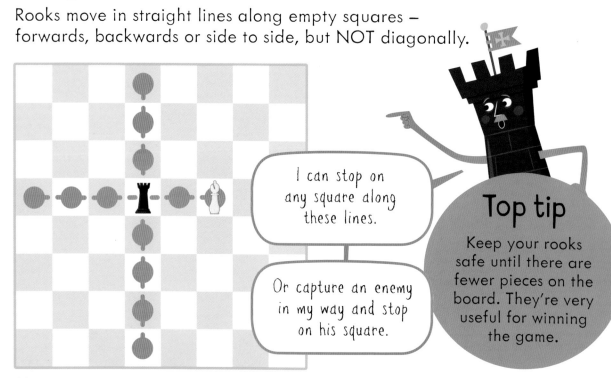

I can stop on any square along these lines.

Or capture an enemy in my way and stop on his square.

## Top tip

Keep your rooks safe until there are fewer pieces on the board. They're very useful for winning the game.

# Castling

A rook can protect its king by using a special move called **castling**, where both pieces jump over each other.

Each player can only castle once in a game, and only if...
- there are no pieces in the way
- the king and rook haven't yet moved
- the king isn't under threat
- the king doesn't move through a square that's under threat.

King, you move two squares this way.

And rook, you move two squares this way.

## Strengths

Rooks are very powerful when there's lots of space on the board.

They can cut off the enemy king and protect their own pieces.

## Weaknesses

Rooks can get stuck behind their own pawns...

...and they are easily threatened by knights and bishops.

Hmm. I appear to be cut off.

You're in my way, pawns.

Go for it, pawn. I've got you covered.

We're going to get you, rook.

19

# The powerful queen

## Many moves

A queen can move in any straight line. She can move sideways, forwards and backwards like a rook, and diagonally like a bishop.

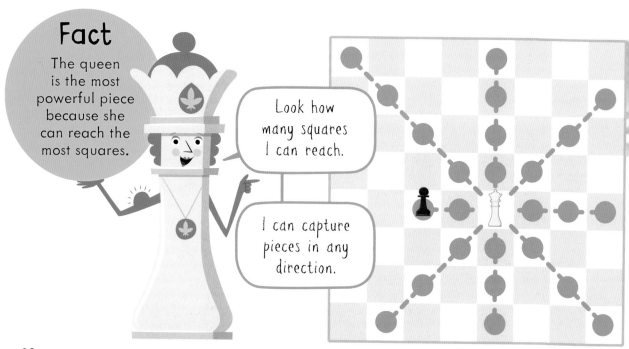

# Strengths

The queen is the strongest attacker on the board, especially when she moves closer to the enemy pieces.

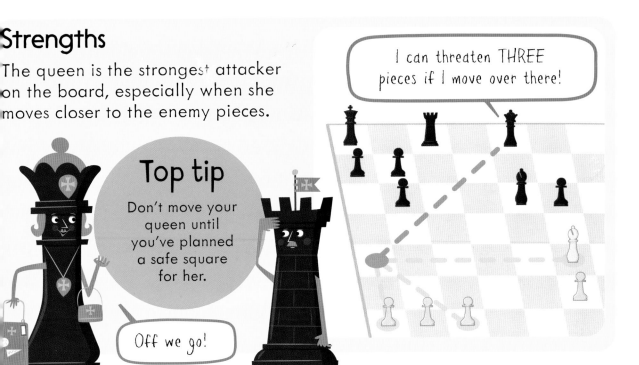

## Top tip

Don't move your queen until you've planned a safe square for her.

*Off we go!*

*I can threaten THREE pieces if I move over there!*

# Weaknesses

The queen doesn't really have a weakness. But because she's so powerful, all the enemy pieces are out to get her!

*I'll block her off here and here.*

*I'll threaten to jump on her while you sneak up the side.*

# Long live the king!

We're the most important pieces on the chess board.

We'd give our lives for you, Your Majesty.

## One step at a time

The king can move in all the same directions as the queen, but only one square at a time. He can capture pieces right next to him.

Which square shall I choose...

You'll need three moves to get here.

Please not this one!

## Top tip

Pawns make useful bodyguards for the king.

# Where to go?

The king CAN'T move onto a square where he could be captured. It's against the rules and it's known as an **illegal move**.

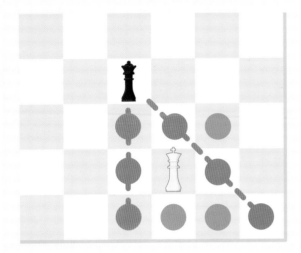

Here, there are only three squares the white king CAN move to.

(On all of the other squares the black queen could capture him next move.)

Now the black rook has joined the attack, there's only one square the king can move to. Can you see which one?

(The other squares are covered by the queen and the rook.)

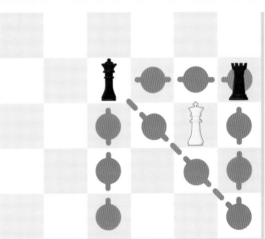

## Fact

You can never have two kings right next to each other.

How did you get here?

One of us has made an illegal move.

# Check and checkmate

You say '**Check**' when you move a piece into a position where it could capture the enemy king next move. You say 'Checkmate' if the king doesn't have a way to escape.

## How to escape check

There are three ways to escape check.

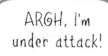

ARGH, I'm under attack!

**1.** Move your king onto a safe square.

Check!

You can't get me now!

**2.** Capture the piece that's threatening the king (either with the king, or with another piece).

Check!

Oh no you don't!

Grrrr.

**3.** Block the threat with another piece.

Check!

You'll have to get me first.

# Is it checkmate?

It can be hard to spot a checkmate. Look for the three ways to escape check. If none of them is possible then sorry, you've lost.

Can you move the king onto a safe square?

Can you capture the attacking piece?

Can you block the attack with another piece?

(You only need one 'yes' to avoid losing.)

## The end

You don't actually move onto the king's square and take the piece off the board. The losing player sometimes lays the king on his side though.

### Fact

'Checkmate!' comes from the Persian words 'Shah mat!' which mean 'The king is helpless!'

Checkmate!

OK, I admit defeat.

# Quick reminder

Before you go into battle, here's a quick reminder of who's who in your army. Each piece has a number of points to show you how valuable it is.

## Pawn

**Pieces at start:** 8
**Value:** 1 point
**Moves:**

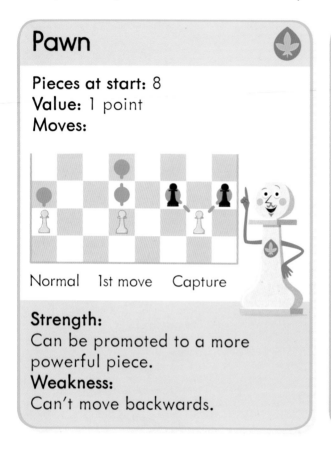

Normal    1st move    Capture

**Strength:**
Can be promoted to a more powerful piece.
**Weakness:**
Can't move backwards.

## Knight

**Pieces at start:** 2
**Value:** 3 points
**Moves:**

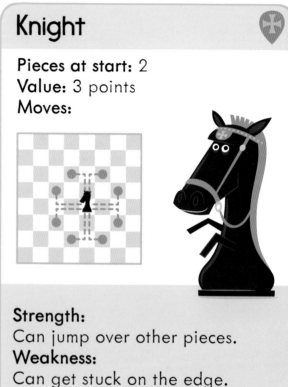

**Strength:**
Can jump over other pieces.
**Weakness:**
Can get stuck on the edge.

## Who's winning?

You can use the points to get an idea of who's winning a game. Count up the points each army has left on the board.

But you'll still need to trap me to win.

My army is slightly in the lead...

 1+9=10

 1+1+1+3+3=9

# Bishop

**Pieces at start:** 2
**Value:** 3 points
**Moves:**

**Strength:**
Can quickly reach all corners of the board.
**Weakness:**
Can't switch from white squares to dark or dark to white.

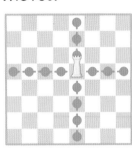

# Rook

**Pieces at start:** 2
**Value:** 5 points
**Moves:**

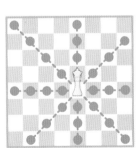

**Strength:**
Can castle to put the king in a safer place.
**Weakness:**
Can't move much until there's space on the board.

# Queen

**Pieces at start:** 1
**Value:** 9 points
**Moves:**

**Strength:**
Can cover the most squares.
**Weakness:**
Always under attack.

# King

**Pieces at start:** 1
**Value:** Priceless!
**Moves:**

**Strength:**
Powerful when there are fewer pieces left on the board.
**Weakness:**
Losing the king loses the game!

# How to start

There are thousands of ways to start a chess game. If you're not careful, things can go wrong pretty quickly! Here are some tips to set you off in the right direction.

Move a few middle pawns first.

Then perhaps a knight or a bishop.

## Fact

Different openings are given different names, such as the Sicilian Dragon or the Fried Liver Attack.*

Don't bring the rooks and queen out too early.

## Top tip

Don't move the same piece more than once at the start, unless you're capturing an enemy piece or avoiding a threat.

Think before you move... or you might regret it!

How's that?

Much safer.

## When should I castle?

Try to castle early on if you can. You'll need to move a pawn, knight and bishop first, then your king can move two squares and your rook can jump over him.

 * There's more about openings on the Usborne Quicklinks website. See p40.

# Aim for the middle

It's a good idea to get your pieces out from their starting positions quickly, so they can take control of the middle squares.

Here, white has made a good start... and black hasn't!

# Attack!

The battle has begun. Now you need to attack the enemy army in order to trap their king. Here are some cunning tricks and traps.

## Forks

A **fork** is when one piece threatens two or more enemy pieces at the same time.

## Skewers

In a **skewer**, one piece also threatens two pieces, but this time the two pieces are one behind the other.

## Pins

**Pins** are like skewers, but the middle piece is less valuable. It has to stay put to protect the more valuable piece.

### Fact

Only queens, bishops and rooks can pin or skewer enemy pieces.

Only one of us can move out of the way...

...so I can capture the other one.

I'd better move to safety...

...but then I'LL get captured!

Help – I'm pinned.

Stay right where you are.

# Surprise!

Your pieces can work together to create surprise attacks.

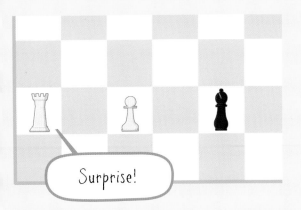

Surprise!

This black bishop looks nice and safe, but what if the pawn moves one square forward...

This is called a **discovered attack**.

What threat is revealed when the white pawn moves? It's called a **discovered check**. The black king will have to move out of check...

Go pawn

Go bishop!

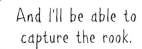

And I'll be able to capture the rook.

Tee hee hee.

Sometimes you can tempt the enemy to capture a piece... then capture a piece of greater value. This is called an uneven **exchange**.

If the black queen captures the rook, what will white do next?

# Defend

As well as attacking, you also need to defend.

## Stay strong

Your army should work as a team, protecting each other and keeping the king safe.

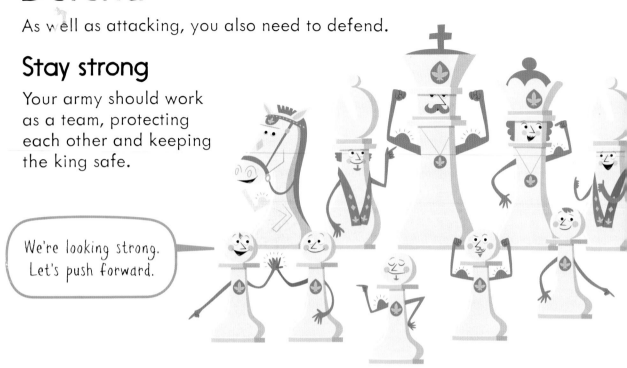

We're looking strong. Let's push forward.

## Backing up

If a piece is under threat, try to back it up with another piece.

See how the black bishop below can back up the black pawn.

Help! White's bishop is after me.

Don't worry, I'll back you up.

Hmm. If the black bishop moves there, I won't be able to capture the pawn without being captured myself.

## Fact

There are really two games going on in chess – what YOU are planning and what your ENEMY is planning.

# Checklist

Here's what you should look for, before you make each move.

## A. Can you get checkmate?

← YES — NO →

Then do it and you've won!

Go to B.

## B. Is your king safe?

← YES — NO →

Go to C.

Then make him safe!

## C. Are your other pieces under attack?

← YES — NO →

Then try to defend them.

Go to D.

## D. Can you safely capture an enemy piece?

← YES — NO →

Then capture it!

Go to E.

## E. Improve your position.

See which of your pieces is in the weakest position and try to make it stronger.

## Top tip

Don't move too quickly. Look at all the possibilities before you reach for a piece.

# Tips on winning

You can win (or lose) a game of chess in only a few moves, but usually it takes much longer. When you're down to just a few pieces on the board, the battle for checkmate really begins...

## Take prisoners

Through the game, aim to capture more pieces than you lose. Then you'll have an advantage.

We're no use now.

## Push through a pawn

Try to promote a pawn to a more powerful piece.

I could do so much more as a queen.

## Corner the king

It's much easier to get checkmate if the king is at the side or in a corner.

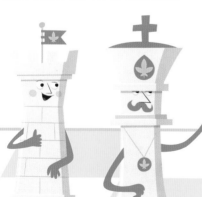

Uh oh, I'm running out of safe squares...

### Top tip

Your own king can play a useful attacking role in the endgame, as long as you're careful.

# Have a plan

It helps to have a checkmate plan. Otherwise you can be chasing the enemy king around the board for ages. Here are some ideas:

# King and queen checkmates

In this checkmate, the white king is protecting the queen.

Here, white's king prevents black's king from escaping the queen.

I can't capture the queen because I'm not allowed next to the white king!

You can't come this way!

## The guillotine

Two rooks (or a rook and a queen) can work together to get checkmate. This is known as the guillotine, because it chops off the king's chance of escape.

## Smothered mate

Sometimes a king can get blocked in, or smothered, by his own pieces. This gives your knight a great chance to get checkmate.

# It's a draw

Lots of chess games end in a draw.
Here are the six ways a draw can happen.

## 1. Stalemate

Stalemate is when your king isn't in check, but there's no move any of your pieces can make without breaking the rules.

Stalemate! It's my move, I'm not in check and I can only move INTO check... so it's a draw.

Oh no – and we were winning.

## 2. Three repeated positions

It's a draw when the exact same position happens three times.

Haven't we been here before?

Yes, twice already. It's a draw.

# 3. Perpetual check

Perpetual means never-ending. If you can keep chasing the enemy king, putting him in check every move, you can force a draw.

# 4. Fifty moves rule

When 50 moves go by without a pawn moving or a piece being captured, then it's also a draw.

# 5. Impossible to win

Some combinations of pieces can't force checkmate, so the result is a draw. The combinations are:

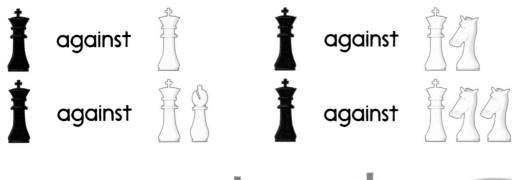

against

against

against

against

# 6. By agreement

Both players can agree to a draw at any time.

Let's call it a draw.

## Top tip

If your opponent offers you a draw, be suspicious. He or she probably thinks you're winning!

S

chess skills with these puzzles. (The answers are on page 40.)

two pieces are in the
starting positions?

B. Which army can castle, white
or black?  black

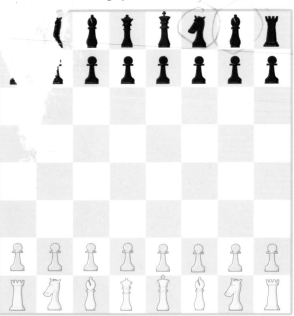

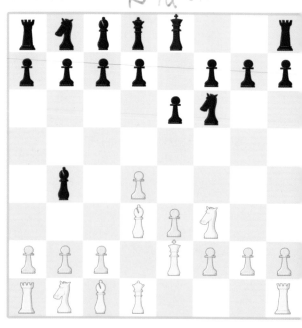

C. What's the best move the
circled pawn could make?

D. How can a white bishop get
checkmate in one move?

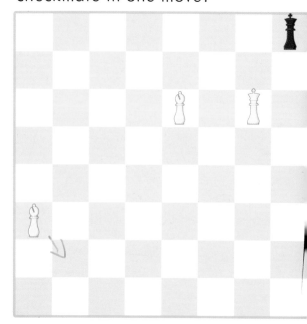

E. Ho... n the black army get
checkmate ... one move?

## More puzzles

For links to more chess puzzles to
solve online or to print out, go to
the Usborne Quicklinks website at
www.usborne.com/quicklinks
and type in the title of this book.

Don't forget to ask a grown-up
before going on the internet.

# Chess word

**castling** – a move where th
goes two squares towards t.
and the rook hops over the ...

**check** – when a king is threat
by an enemy piece.

**checkmate** – when there's no
way for a king to escape che...
Checkmate ends the game.

**discovered attack/check** – an a...ck
or check that's revealed when
another piece moves out of the way.

**exchange** – when the two players
capture each other's pieces.

**fork** – when two or more pieces
are attacked at the same time.

**illegal move** – a move that's
against the rules.

**opening** – the pattern of moves
at the beginning of a game.

**perpetual check** – when a king
is put in check on every move but
can't be checkmated. It's a draw.

**pin** – an attack on a piece that's
shielding one of greater value.

**promotion** – when a pawn reaches
the other end and is replaced with
a more powerful piece.

**skewer** – an attack that forces a
valuable piece to move, exposing
one of less value to attack.

**stalemate** – when the player whose
turn it is can't move but isn't in
check. It's a draw.

# Answers and credits

Here are the answers to the puzzles on pages 38 and 39.

A. The black bishop and knight on the right have changed places.

B. Black can castle. (White can't – its king has already moved.)

C. Capture the black pawn (to stop it from reaching the edge of the board and getting promoted).

D. The white bishop on the dark square can move diagonally down one square to the right.

E. The black king just moves one square up, creating a discovered check by the queen. The white king can't escape. Checkmate!

## About the author

Katie Daynes was taught to play chess by her son, Joe Birks, who became the British Under 9 Chess Champion in 2017. She hasn't beaten him for a few years now, but her game is still improving.

## About the expert

Sarah Hegarty became the British Ladies Chess Champion in 2013. She's been coaching junior chess players since 2015 and now runs the world's biggest chess competition, the UK Schools' Chess Challenge.

Edited by Sam Taplin
Internet research by Jacqui Clarke